Looking After My Eyes

Sheila Hollins, Stephen Kill, Scott Watkin and Maggie Woodhou
illustrated by Beth Webb

Beyond Words

London

3

11

Looking After My Eyes

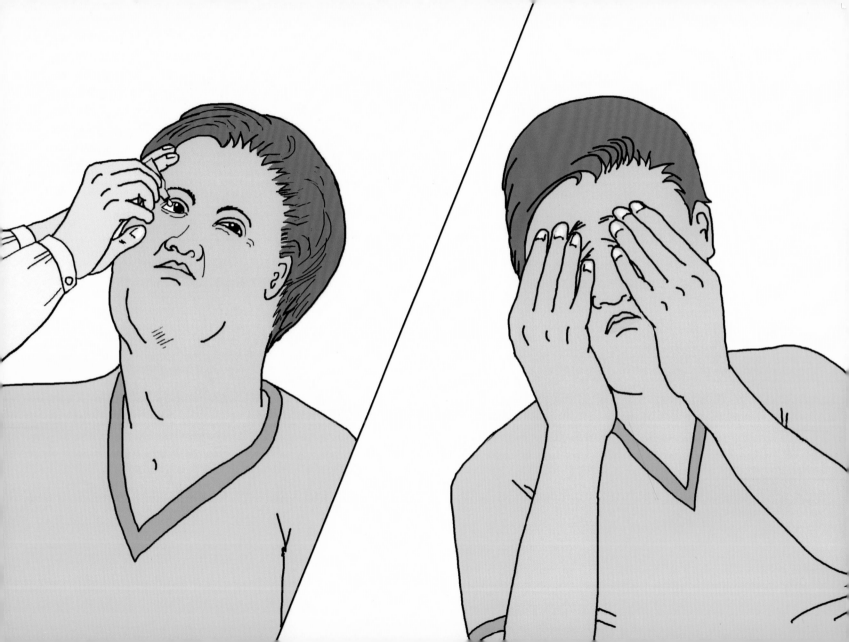

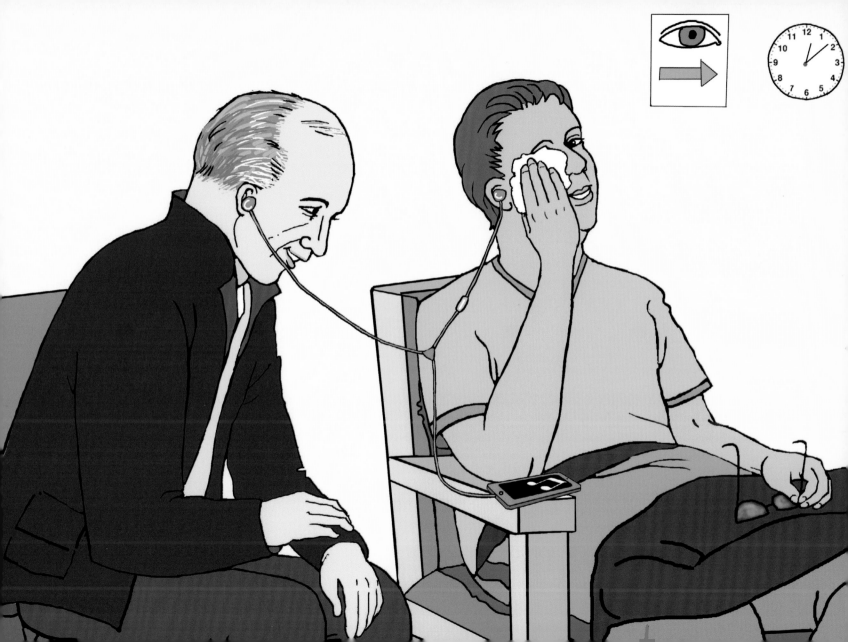

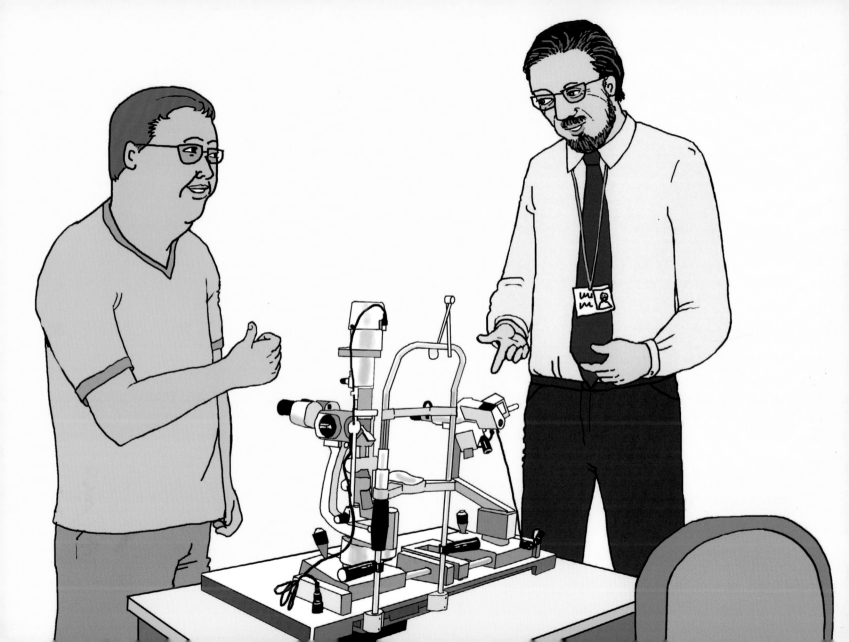

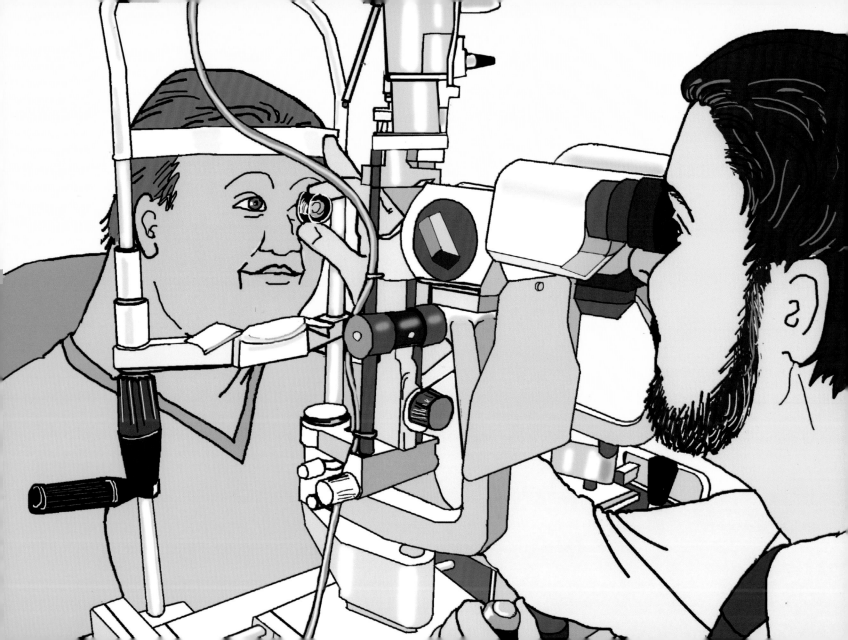

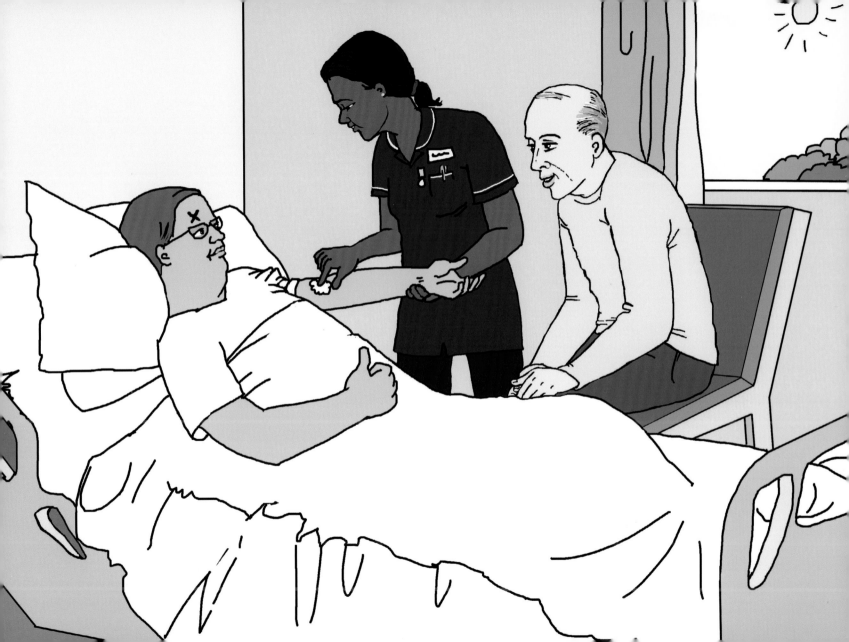

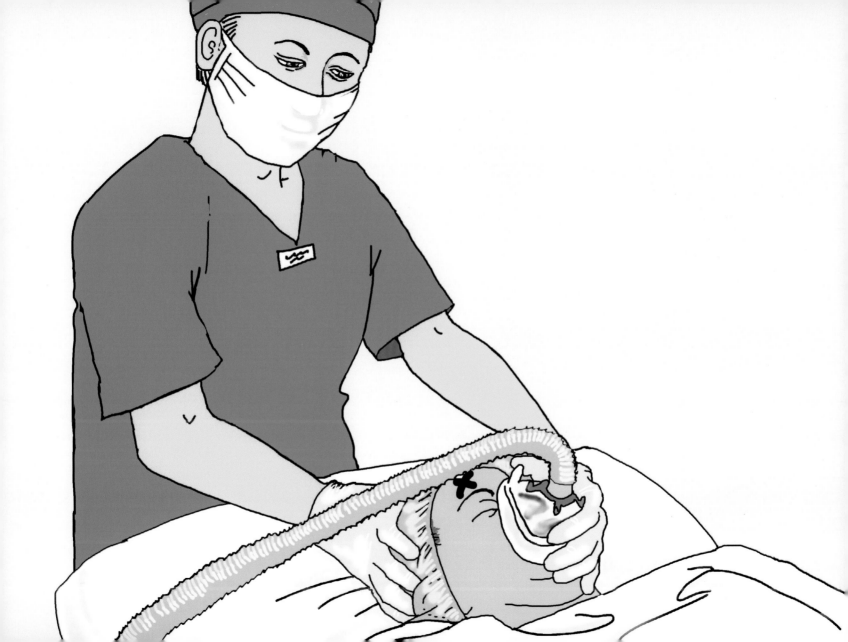

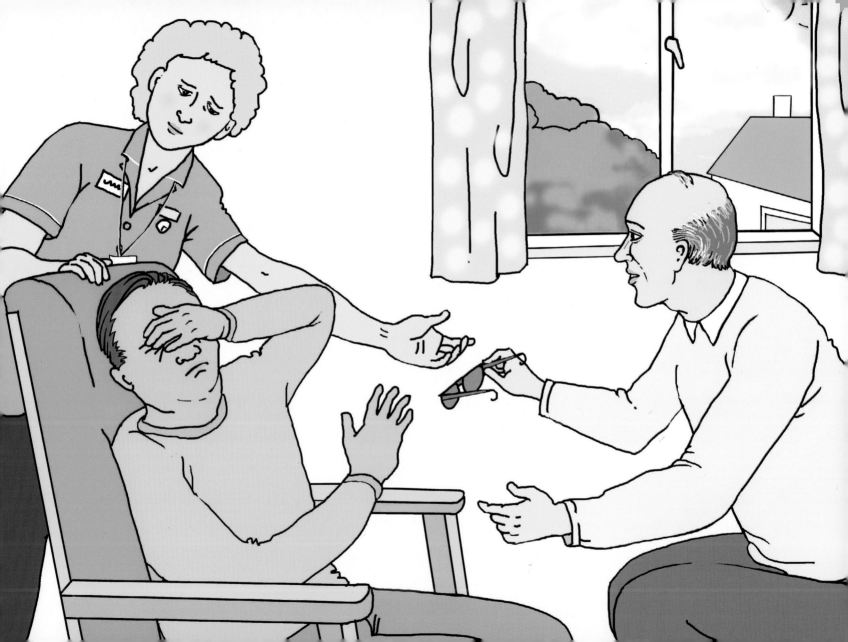

34

37

First published in the UK 2019 by Books Beyond Words.

Text & illustrations © Books Beyond Words, 2019.

No part of this book may be reproduced in any form, or by any means, without the prior permission in writing from the publisher.

ISBN 978-1-78458-110-7

British Library Cataloguing-in-Publication Data

A catalogue record for this book is available from the British Library.

Printed by Blackmore Group, Shaftesbury.

Books Beyond Words is a Charitable Incorporated Organisation (no. 1183942).

Further information about the Books Beyond Words series can be obtained from Beyond Words' website: www.booksbeyondwords.co.uk.

Who is this book for?

This book is for anyone who finds pictures easier to understand than words. People with learning disabilities are currently the main group of people finding the book useful. In the UK we talk about someone having a 'learning disability', or sometimes 'learning difficulty'. 'Intellectual disability', 'intellectual developmental disability' or 'mental handicap' are terms that people use in other parts of the world.

Someone with a learning disability may find it hard to understand new or complex information and to learn new skills. They may need support to live as independently as they choose. Their condition will have started before adulthood and have a lasting impact on their life.

Having a learning disability does not mean that a person is not capable of understanding the advice, support or treatment they are given. Many people will be able to understand a situation more easily and make good decisions with the help of the pictures in this book. Some may benefit from just one or two well-chosen pictures. Others will need extra time and support to understand information, whether presented in simplified language or non-verbally.

Other people will find the picture stories in Books Beyond Words useful too:
- people with other cognitive or communication difficulties, such as dementia
- people who have difficulty with reading, including some Deaf people
- people who do not use the language of the country where they are living.

Contents

Storyline

The following words are provided for readers and supporters who want some ideas about one possible story. Most readers make their own story up from the pictures.

1. Fiona is going to the library. She can't see very well. That's why she has a white cane.

2. Fiona meets her book club friends.

3. Jade says, "I can't see everything in the pictures". Fiona says, "Do you need glasses?"

4. Sylvie and Jade go to the opticians. Sylvie says, "I know you're a bit scared but I'm here for you."

5. Jade gives her appointment letter to the receptionist.

6. She goes in for her eye test. The optometrist asks her to sit in the chair.

7. She asks Jade, "What can you see?" The pictures look blurred to Jade.

8. Now the optometrist is looking into her eye with a light.

9. The optometrist shows Jade some frames she must put on. She will try different lenses in the frames to find the right ones for Jade.

10. The light is off. The optometrist is using a light to check Jade's eyes.

11. Jade is wearing the frames. The optometrist puts different bits of glass in the frame. She tries to find the right lenses for her.

12. Jade says, "I can see better now."

13. This is the fun bit! She tries on lots of different glasses. The optician helps her to choose.

14. Jade goes back to collect her glasses. The optician checks that they fit well.

15. Jade is at home with Sylvie and her cat. She has her new glasses on. She can read much better now.

16. Jade goes back to the book club. "Hi everybody! Do you like my glasses?"

17. Everyone looks concerned as Mac seems to have a problem seeing.

18. He can see the picture with a magnifying glass. Fiona tells him, "You can get your eyes tested too, just like Jade."

19. Mac goes to the hospital with John.

20. Mac and John wait in the eye clinic's waiting room.

21. "Hi Mac, I'm Doctor McTavish. Come this way, follow me," says the doctor.

22. Mac has some drops put in his eyes. His eyes sting! But it only stings for a minute.

23. He has to wait for the drops to work. While they wait Mac listens to music with John.

24. The doctor explains the machine to Mac and how he is going to look at his eyes. "Please rest your chin on here," the doctor says.

25. The doctor looks in Mac's eye.

26. The doctor shows Mac a picture about the operation he wants to do. Mac asks some questions.

27. Mac is making his mind up.

28. Mac is in the hospital. Today is his operation.

29. Now he is asleep and has a tube in his mouth to help him breathe during the operation.

30. The operation is over, and Mac is back on the ward. He enjoys a cup of tea.

31. Mac and John go home in the car. It's raining. Mac has a bandage to cover his eye.

32. The nurse comes to take off the bandage.

33. Mac covers his eyes from the bright sunlight.

34. Mac says, "I can see. Thank you. The operation worked."

35. Mac and John watch football on television. He looks happy – he can follow the ball better now.

36. Mac is back at the book group. He doesn't need a magnifying glass now.

37. They do a jigsaw together, for a change.

Why is eye care important?

It is estimated that you receive more information from your eyes than from any of your other senses. Your sight helps you to communicate, move around safely and make sense of your surroundings. Vision stimulates you to explore the world around you and to learn new skills. You need to make the best use of the sight that you have.

You need to look after your eyes and you cannot assume that they will always be healthy. It is important you get good eye care because some eye problems can lead to sight loss. Good eyesight helps you to do things for yourself. Poor eyesight makes this more difficult and means that you may need more help from others.

Some people are more likely to have sight problems than other people. This includes:

- people with learning disabilities

- people with diabetes

- people who have someone with glaucoma in their family

- older people.

For example, adults with learning disabilities are 10 times more likely to have serious sight problems than other people.

What are the signs of having a sight problem?

Eyesight problems can affect anyone at any age. You may not be aware that you have poor eyesight or that your vision is changing. Also some disabled people may find it difficult to tell someone else if they are concerned about their eyes or not able to see very well.

This means that carers and supporters have a very important role to play in helping people to look after their eyes.

Here are some signs for carers and supporters to look out for which may suggest that someone is having problems with their vision.

- Does the person bump into things when they move around?

- Do they knock things over on the table?

- Do they bring things close to their face to look at them or screw their eyes up?

- Do they shield their eyes from bright sunlight?

- Do their eyes look red or watery?

- Has their behaviour changed, such as becoming withdrawn or not enjoying their usual activities?

If you think that someone is having problems with their vision, book an eye test soon rather than waiting for their next scheduled appointment.

How can you look after your eyes?

The best way to look after your eyes is to have an eye test. Adults should have an eye test every two years or more often if needed. Eye tests are usually carried out at an optician's practice but it can be done at home if you need this.

The person who helps you to look after your eyes is called an optician and there are two types. An optometrist checks how well you can see, whether your eyes are healthy and tells you if you need to wear glasses to see more clearly. A dispensing optician helps you choose the right glasses and makes sure you have the correct type of lens and that your glasses fit you properly. Both optometrists and dispensing opticians can advise you about magnifiers and contact lenses.

You can go to any optician's practice – you can choose.

Having an eye test can be quite an ordeal for some people. You may feel anxious about having your eyes checked and about all the different tests that the optometrist does.

There are lots of things that can be done to support you to have a good eye test. Sometimes these are called 'reasonable adjustments' (see page 47).

Before the appointment

- Your family or support worker can talk to you about the eye test and about what is going to happen.

- You can ask to visit the practice in advance so that you are familiar with the environment.

- You can think about whether you prefer to use letters or pictures at the eye test and whether you will say them, match the pictures, or do Makaton signing. The optometrist can still check your eyes even if you are not able to tell them what you can see or you can't name, match or sign letters or pictures.

- You can practise at home with one eye covered, naming letters or pictures and having someone look very closely at your eyes before the day of the eye test.

- Fill in SeeAbility's "Telling the optometrist about me" form in advance and give this to the optometrist, so they can tailor the test to suit you.

At the appointment

- When the optometrist is looking at your eyes, sometimes the lights will be turned off for a short time. In our pictures, we have left the lights on so that you can see what's going on. If you are afraid of the dark, don't forget to tell the optometrist beforehand.

- If you go with someone, ask them to help you communicate with the optometrist.

- You can tell the optometrist if you need more time or need them to explain something in a different way.

- You can ask the optometrist to fill in SeeAbility's "Feedback from my optometrist" form so that you can understand the results of your eye test.

After the appointment

- Talk to your carers about the feedback form so you understand what has happened.

- Share the results with other people who are involved in your support.

- If you get glasses, your carers will support you to wear the glasses, keep them clean and get them adjusted when they don't fit properly. Opticians usually adjust glasses for free.

If you need to be seen at the hospital about your eyes, your optometrist or your GP will make the arrangements. In an emergency, you can go directly to A&E, but otherwise see your optometrist or GP first.

A guide for health care staff on reasonable adjustments

The Equality Act 2010 requires services in England and Wales to make 'reasonable adjustments' to support all people with protected characteristics to make full use of their service. This includes people with learning disabilities and people with autism. The Act also specifies that services must anticipate and plan for the needs of people with protected characteristics when considering what adjustments to make, rather than simply reacting to needs as they are presented.

Attending to patients with learning disabilities can take more time. Some people may find it very difficult to be kept waiting. They may need a double appointment to assess their needs or more than one appointment to familiarise themselves with a proposed test or procedure beforehand. They may need their family or support worker to be with them in the consulting room. Other examples of reasonable adjustments include:

- providing relevant information in a form that the patient understands, such as the pictures in this book

- changing the physical environment, for example by using a quiet room with fewer distractions and stresses

- offering the first or last appointment to minimise their time in the waiting area

- providing a higher staffing level to meet the patient's additional needs

- putting message alerts on the patient's electronic record so that everybody who sees them knows about their specific needs and appropriate reasonable adjustments.

If health care staff are worried about meeting the needs of patients with learning disabilities, they can contact their local Community Learning Disability Team for advice (CLDT, see page 56). If a patient is known to the CLDT, the team can often provide advice and assistance relating to that person, or more general training to health care staff on how to meet the needs of patients with learning disabilities.

Wearing glasses

If you are prescribed glasses, the dispensing optician should explain whether you need to wear glasses for near tasks, distance vision or all the time. They should give you advice on how you can get used to wearing glasses. It is very important that you receive good support to wear them. Relatives and supporters who wear glasses should take a moment to think how their own life would be different if they didn't have their glasses every day.

Getting the first pair of glasses can be a challenge for anyone, even if you do understand why you need to wear them. Some people will need support to understand why and when they should wear their glasses. It can take a while for wearing glasses to become part of your routine. You may not be comfortable wearing them for long periods straight away. A consistent approach over time by all of your supporters will be really helpful. More information is available on the SeeAbility website (see page 56).

It's important to keep your glasses clean

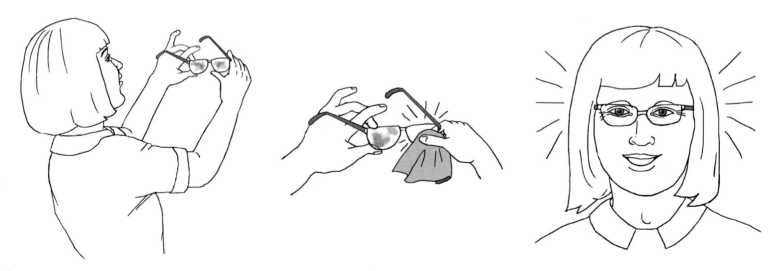

Eye conditions and surgery

If you have an eye condition, it is very important that you are diagnosed as soon as possible. This will help you to get the right treatment at the right time. You may need to see an eye doctor, known as an ophthalmologist. This usually happens in a hospital eye clinic. As with an eye test, there are lots of reasonable adjustments that can be made to make the appointment more accessible for you.

If you have an eye clinic appointment, it is important that you receive good support to prepare for, attend and understand the results of your appointment.

You can ask for information to help you understand more about your condition. You can request information in a format that is accessible to you. Some people like easy read information with pictures.

At the appointment, the ophthalmologist will examine your eyes. They will tell you if there is any treatment or an operation that will help you. You should be given support to decide if you want to have treatment or an operation. You can get support from your family, friends, support staff, an advocate or a nurse. If you want to have treatment or surgery, you should be given the chance to have this. If you cannot make the decision, this can be discussed at a Best Interests meeting with the help of people who know you well.

If you have a problem with your vision, here are some useful questions for you or your supporter to ask:

1. What is the name of my eye condition?

2. Do you have information about my eye condition in an accessible format that I can understand?

3. Is there any treatment for my eye condition and what does this involve?

4. If I do not have any treatment, what will happen to my vision?

The hospital may give you an appointment to come back. It is important to carry on with your regular eye tests, as well as your hospital eye clinic visits.

Eye drops

When you have your eyes examined, the optometrist or ophthalmologist may need to put drops in your eyes. All drops sting a little bit when they go in, but only for a few moments.

Sometimes drops are used to numb your eyes, some change the colour of your tears to make problems easier to see. Both of these wear off very quickly.

Another type of drop is used to widen your pupils and allow the examiner to get a really good look at the inside of your eye. These drops take a long time to take effect so expect to have to wait quite a while. The darker your eyes the longer the drops take to work, so it might be a good idea to take something to do while you are in the waiting room. The drops may make your vision blurred, so don't take a book; try some music that you can listen to on headphones. These drops also take a long time to wear off and might mean that sunlight is a bit uncomfortable – take sunglasses or a large hat with you if you're worried about this.

Living with sight problems

If you do have a sight problem that cannot be helped with glasses or an operation, it does not mean that you have to stop doing things for yourself. With the right support, you can still do the things that you enjoy.

If you do have sight loss, your family and supporters need to know how much you can see, so they can give you the support you need. You may need to see things close up or you may have better vision in one eye. You can write information about your eyes in a Vision Passport (see page 56, under SeeAbility) and show it to your family and supporters.

If your sight is poor, the ophthalmologist may give you a certificate to say that you are sight-impaired/ partially sighted or that you are severely sight-impaired/ blind. This means that you can be registered with social services and may be able to get more help. If you're blind it doesn't always mean you have no sight at all. Some people who are registered blind can still see enough to read and to get around.

You can ask for a visit from a Rehabilitation Worker who works with people with sight loss. The Rehabilitation Worker can help you to learn new ways of doing things for yourself. Sometimes they can show you different kinds of enabling equipment that can help and sometimes they can teach you new skills.

For example, over the next three pages there are some illustrations showing a liquid level indicator as an example of enabling equipment.

In the pictures, Fiona is making a drink but she cannot see this very well because she has poor vision. As she pours the kettle, water overflows the cup and spills onto the table top. Anne and Bill notice and want to help.

Bill shows Fiona a device called a liquid level indicator. Bill places the liquid level indicator over the edge of the cup. Fiona pours the kettle and when the water reaches the liquid level indicator, the device makes a bleeping noise. Fiona knows that now she should stop pouring, and that no water has been spilt.

Liquid level indicators can be bought from RNIB (see page 56) and many local sight loss charities.

People who can help

Optometrist
This is the person who gives you an eye test. They check your eyesight and whether your eye is healthy.

Dispensing optician
They have had special training to help you choose the right glasses and make sure they fit properly.

Ophthalmologist
This is the eye doctor who works at the hospital eye clinic. They can give medicines and do surgery on people with some eye problems to try and make them better.

Orthopist
They also work at the hospital eye clinic and measure what you can see and how your eyes work together.

Learning disability nurse
They work in community or hospital teams and can help people with learning disabilities who may need extra support with eye care.

Rehabilitation Worker
They work with adults who have sight loss. They train people in everyday skills and can show you useful equipment.

Habilitation Worker
They do the same role as a Rehabilitation Worker but they work with children and young adults who have sight loss.

Useful resources in the UK

Services

SeeAbility
The national charity SeeAbility is working for inclusive communities where people with sight loss, autism, and learning disabilities participate as equal citizens. It has a range of factsheets and resources about eye care for people with learning disabilities. It also has a list of optometrists and dispensing opticians who have shared information on their services for people with learning disabilities. SeeAbility resources mentioned in this book:
* *Telling the optometrist about me*
* *Feedback from my optometrist*
* *Vision Passport*

www.seeability.org
Tel: 01372 755 000

Community Learning Disability Teams (CLDTs)
These are specialist multidisciplinary health teams that support adults with learning disabilities and their families by assessment of their health needs and a range of clinical interventions. The composition of CLDTs varies, but will usually include psychology, psychiatry and nursing with a range of therapeutic specialists such as speech and language therapy, occupational therapy and physiotherapy. Referral to the local CLDT is encouraged for both developmental and therapeutic work. Some are joint health and social work teams and have a social care management role as well.

RNIB
The Royal National Institute of Blind People (RNIB) offer support to people with sight loss and information about eye conditions. It has a shop where you can buy a liquid level indicator and other useful equipment.
www.rnib.org.uk
Helpline: 0303 123 9999

Local sight loss charities

These organisations provide support for people who have sight loss around the country. Some of these organisations provide opportunities to buy useful equipment or to meet other people with sight loss. You can find your nearest sight loss charity on the Visionary website.

www.visionary.org.uk

Helpline: 020 8090 9264

Rehabilitation Workers

They work with people who have sight loss. They can be based with social services or a local sight loss charity. You can find your nearest Rehabilitation Worker on the Sightline directory.

www.sightlinedirectory.org.uk

College of Optometrists

This is the professional body for optometrists.

www.college-optometrists.org

Tel: 020 7839 6000

Association of British Dispensing Opticians

ABDO is the professional body for dispensing opticians.

www.abdo.org.uk

Tel: 01227 733905

Information and materials available online

NHS Choices list of opticians services

www.nhs.uk/service-search/Opticians/LocationSearch/9

Free NHS eye tests and optical vouchers information

www.nhs.uk/NHSEngland/Healthcosts/Pages/Eyecarecosts.aspx

Easy Health
A website that provides easy to read leaflets on all sorts of health and other issues, including eye problems.
www.easyhealth.org.uk

Ophthalmic Services Guidance: Eye Care for Adults with Learning Disabilities. Guidance published by the Royal College of Ophthalmologists to help eye care professionals provide good quality treatment to patients with learning disabilities.
www.rcophth.ac.uk/wp-content/uploads/2015/09/Eye-Care-Services-for-Adults-with-Learning-Disabilities.pdf

Related titles in the Books Beyond Words series

Going to the Doctor (2018, 2nd edition) by Sheila Hollins, Jane Bernal and Dominic Slowie, illustrated by Beth Webb. This book illustrates a variety of experiences which may occur during a visit to the GP. These include meeting the doctor, having one's ears syringed, a physical examination, a blood test, a blood pressure check and getting a prescription.

Going into Hospital (2015, 2nd edition) by Sheila Hollins, Angie Avis and Samantha Cheverton, with Jim Blair, illustrated by Denise Redmond. This book helps to prepare and support people being admitted to hospital, by explaining what happens, covering planned admission and accident and emergency.

Going to Out-Patients (2017, 2nd edition) by Sheila Hollins, Jane Bernal and Matthew Gregory, illustrated by Denise Redmond. This book explains what happens in out-patient departments, covering tests such as ultrasound, x-ray and hearing tests.

Getting on with Type 1 Diabetes (2012) by Sheila Hollins and Rachel Besser, illustrated by Catherine Brighton. Florence is always thirsty and lacks energy. She is referred to hospital and has lots of tests. She is told she has diabetes and learns how to inject insulin and eat a healthy diet.

Getting on with Type 2 Diabetes (2012) by Sheila Hollins, Rachel Besser, Libby Dowling and Charles Fox, illustrated by Catherine Brighton. Louise is alarmed when Fred keeps falling asleep. His GP diagnoses type 2 diabetes. He is shown how to change his diet and take regular exercise, and we see him cooking and eating a healthy meal. Later on, medication helps him to manage his diabetes.

Going to the Dentist (2016) by Sheila Hollins, Amber Qureshi and Lloyd Page, illustrated by Beth Webb. Matthew eats lots of sugary foods and doesn't take very good care of his teeth. When Matthew gets toothache he goes to see the dentist where he agrees to have a check-up and treatment. Matthew also learns from the dentist how to keep his teeth and gums healthy.

Authors and artist

Sheila Hollins is Emeritus Professor of Psychiatry of Disability at St George's, University of London, and sits in the House of Lords. She is a past President of the Royal College of Psychiatrists and of the BMA. She is the founder, lead editor and Executive Chair of Beyond Words, and a family carer.

Stephen Kill is a qualified Rehabilitation Worker with people who have a visual impairment. He works for SeeAbility to increase access to eye care and vision services for people with learning disabilities.

Scott Watkin BEM works for SeeAbility, campaigning for the rights of people with learning disabilities including access to eye care. Previously, Scott was co-national director for people with learning disabilities.

J Margaret (Maggie) Woodhouse is an optometrist and Senior Lecturer at Cardiff University, where she has a research, clinical and teaching interest in eye care for children and adults with learning disability.

Beth Webb is the artist who helped to develop the concept of Books Beyond Words in its early days. She is also the author of 14 novels for children and young people and is a professional storyteller.

Acknowledgments

We are grateful for the advice and support of our advisory group: Linda Allchorne, Karen Card, Celia Chandler, Amanda Cresswell, Lisa Donaldson, Nigel Hollins, Jayne Jazz, Grace McGill, Vivian Namagembe, Rachel Pilling, Adam Southworth, Jo Ticehurst, Alicia Wood and Hugo Wookey.

Many thanks to Alexander Ionides, Moorfields Eye Hospital, for his help in the early stages, and all individuals and groups who trialled the pictures, including Plymouth People First – PLUSS: Zoe O'Connor, Debbie Howlett, Tina Oxan and Chas Jane Broguh; Ivan Storey, Laura Marshall, Shay Young and others supported by SeeAbility; Lisa Donaldson; Talk 2 Us: Paula Lowson and Peter Gardiner; Meg and Emily, supported by Dimensions; Tricuro Day Service – Weymouth Connect at the Acorns: Angie, Julia, Ria and Abi; MacIntyre I4T (Inspired for Training), Chesterfield Group: Heather, Kim, Sharon, Christine, Alan and supporters Alison and

Carole; Southern Health Foundation Trust: Basingstoke Speak Out Group Southern Health, Southampton Service User Group and Winchester Service User Group, James Elsworthy and Rosie Batty; Advocacy for All, Bromley Together: Laura Frewin, Polly Sharpey, Kate Rosie, Gillian Rees, Gordon Ager, Teresa Durman, Sylvia Hicks, Annie Parsons, Joanne Gifford, Martin Tooley, George Manwaring, Linda Allchorne and Matthew Froude. Supporters: Dave Norgate, Jackie Allen and Chris King; Ian Robinson supported by Rachel Pilling, Bradford Teaching Hospitals; Bexley Mencap, Respect in Bexley.

Finally, we are grateful to SeeAbility's loyal supporters for their generous financial support of this book.

Beyond Words: publications and training

Books Beyond Words are stories for anyone who finds pictures easier than words. A list of all Beyond Words publications, including print and eBook versions of Books Beyond Words titles, and where to buy them, can be found on our website:

www.booksbeyondwords.co.uk

Workshops co-taught by trainers with learning disabilities for family carers, support workers and professionals can be provided on request. Self-advocates are always welcome. E-learning modules about using Books Beyond Words will also be useful for some people. For information about training and e-learning, please contact us:

email: admin@booksbeyondwords.co.uk

Video clips showing our books being read are also on our website and YouTube channel: www.youtube.com/user/booksbeyondwords.

How to read this book

This is a story for people who find pictures easier to understand than words. It is not necessary to be able to read any words at all.

1. Some people are not used to reading books. Start at the beginning and read the story in each picture. Encourage the reader to hold the book themselves and to turn the pages at their own pace.

2. Whether you are reading the book with one person or with a group, encourage them to tell the story in their own words. You will discover what each person thinks is happening, what they already know, and how they feel. You may think something different is happening in the pictures yourself, but that doesn't matter. Wait to see if their ideas change as the story develops. Don't challenge the reader(s) or suggest their ideas are wrong.

3. Some pictures may be more difficult to understand. It can help to prompt the people you are supporting, for example:

   - I wonder who that is?

   - I wonder what is happening?

   - What is he or she doing now?

   - I wonder how he or she is feeling?

   - Do you feel like that? Has it happened to you/ your friend/ your family?

4. You don't have to read the whole book in one sitting. Allow people enough time to follow the pictures at their own pace.

5. Some people will not be able to follow the story, but they may be able to understand some of the pictures. Stay a little longer with the pictures that interest them.